Once Upon A Dream

Worlds Of Wonder

Edited By Jess Giaffreda

First published in Great Britain in 2019 by:

Young Writers
Remus House
Coltsfoot Drive
Peterborough
PE2 9BF
Telephone: 01733 890066
Website: www.youngwriters.co.uk

All Rights Reserved
Book Design by Ashley Janson
© Copyright Contributors 2019
Softback ISBN 978-1-83928-047-4
Hardback ISBN 978-1-83928-048-1
Printed and bound in the UK by BookPrintingUK
Website: www.bookprintinguk.com
YB0419W

THE POEMS

FOREWORD

Welcome Reader, to a world of dreams.
For Young Writers' latest competition, we asked our writers to dig deep into their imagination and create a poem that paints a picture of what they dream of, whether it's a make-believe world full of wonder or their aspirations for the future.
The result is this collection of fantastic poetic verse that covers a whole host of different topics. Let your mind fly away with the fairies to explore the sweet joy of candy lands, join in with a game of fantasy football, or you may even catch a glimpse of a unicorn or another mythical creature. Beware though, because even dreamland has dark corners, so you may turn a page and walk into a nightmare!
Whereas the majority of our writers chose to stick to a free verse style, others gave themselves the challenge of other techniques such as acrostics and rhyming couplets. We also gave the writers the option to compose their ideas in a story, so watch out for those narrative pieces too!
Each piece in this collection shows the writers' dedication and imagination – we truly believe that seeing their work in print gives them a well-deserved boost of pride, and inspires them to keep writing, so we hope to see more of their work in the future!

CONTENTS

Independent Entries

Dawud Alshameri (11)	1
Nicole Carmen Stoicescu (10)	2
Maryam Rafi	5
Maryam Khanom (8)	6
Holly Dimery (11)	8
Eunice Opemipo Olagbolabo (10)	10
Aqsa Ali	12
Breanna Obeng (11)	14
Jaimee Luspo (10)	16
Abishan Jesuthas	18
Megan Rosemary Neale (10)	20
Savannah Williston (7)	22
Jack William Machin (10)	24
Tvisha Lakshmeesh	26
Ayaan Saqib (9)	28
Ayomide David Ajayi (10)	30
Haniya Hanif (11)	32
Rithika Raghunandanan (7)	34
Kaitlyn Weir (10)	36
Harry Cheesman (7)	38
Temiloluwa Emmanuel Kalejaiye (9)	40
Catriona MacKinnon	42
Kaitlin Elizabeth Grafton (11)	43
Chanelle Gatheru (11)	44
Joshua Nahmad	46
Poppy Alice Smeeton	48
Fara Adesakin (8)	50
Tayla Brady (10)	51
Katie Thornton (6)	52
Emily Agha Mohammad Zadeh (10)	54
Victoria Mmesoma Nwachukwu (10)	55
Sophie Gelder (10)	56
Abby-Lee Cliffe	57
Oluwatamilore Gabriel Kalejaiye (10)	58
Ray Marcou (10)	59
Lexie Elina Sabatelli (9)	60
Anoushka Apte (10)	61
Princess Ahmed	62
Allena Vincatassin (10)	64
Izabel Cliffe	65
Jack Hei Lee (10)	66
Alexandra Rosemary Isabella Woods	67
Mya (7)	68
Connor Sado (11)	69
William John Henry Reavill (9)	70
Khadija Saleh	71
Hajra Jamshed (10)	72
Lachlan Lasikiewicz (10)	73
Haniyah Iman Yaqub (10)	74
Ellie Wong (8)	76
Amber Clements	77
Summer Samantha Green (10)	78
Alisha Taylor (10)	79
Hirah Khan	80
Aish Sarmad	81
Daniel Martin Haynes (9)	82
Kamy Patel (10)	83
Munashe Whitlam Mazenge (9)	84
Harshita Srihari (7)	85
Fiorella (7)	86
Onur Hurriyetoglu (8)	87
Sophia Wretham	88
Teghvir Singh	89
Naomi Lily Stanyer (11)	90
Muhammad-Abdisalam Ahmed	91

Mia Sahni (10)	92
Lara Hardee Dorsett (8)	93
Olivia Prendergast	94
Ziyue Zhou (9)	95
Bethany Wretham	96
Ayomide Deborah Aboyeji (10)	97
Chloe Jaidon Weedon (10)	98
Chudi Patrick Onwuokwu (8)	99
Hibbah Altaf	100
Keeley Grant	101
Carys Hunt	102
Terence Noble	103
Tyler Dunn	104
AJ Yates	105

Anahilt Primary School, Hillsborough

Georgia Wilson (10)	106
Abigail Weatherhead (10)	108
Olivia Margaret Dodds (11)	109
Cassidy McMullan (10)	110
Ellie Sloan (9)	111
Dawn Erwin (10)	112
Matthew Patterson (9)	113
Henry Houston (9)	114
Rachel Douglas (9)	115
Erin Burns (9)	116
Ellie Wright (10)	117
Nathan Mitchell (9)	118
Jacob Wilson (10)	119
Camilla McMullan (9)	120
Oliver Kinnear (10)	121
Cian Suitor (8)	122
Tilly Vaughan (9)	123
Katie Rutherford (10)	124
Thomas Reid (10)	125
Caitlyn Gillian Patterson (10)	126
Rauri Liam Toland (10)	127

Ballymagee Primary School, Bangor

Mia Hegarty (9)	128

Bright Futures School, Greenacres

Henry Graeme Crowther (11)	129

Brookfield Special School, Moira

Reece Orr (10)	130
Charlie Irwin (10)	131

Corran Integrated Primary School, Larne

Daniel Thomas Lloyd (10)	132
Lucy O'Cleary (10)	133
Evelyn Donnelly (10)	134

Field View Primary School, Bilston

Isabella Sophia Cantrill Taylor (9)	135
Sirafima Bubnovska (9)	136
Marlon Dalton Bowen (9)	138
Trey Smith (9)	139
Evie Cart (8)	140
Lijana Liutvinskyte (9)	141
Wiktoria Oliwia Jaramek (9)	142
Adrian Philip Brzezinski (9)	143
Debina Chander (9)	144
Izan Duque (9)	145
Sukhraj Jakhu (9)	146
Jannati Robia (9)	147
Veerjyot Singh (9)	148
Sofia Bubnovska (9)	149
Tyreece Davis (9)	150
Gurparteek Singh Shergill (9)	151
Tallia Jane Lewis (9)	152
Kelsie Lydia Shirley (8)	153
Ammaar Binasif (9)	154
Lexi Pearson (9)	155
Emilija Zurauskaite (9)	156
Paige Parkes (9)	157
Hareet Kaur Randhawa (9)	158
Cobey Dean (9)	159
Nihal Dhaliwal (9)	160
Jugraaj Kler (9)	161

Grace Parsons (9)	162
Zechariah Parkash (9)	163
Iovondeep (8)	164
Lloyd Harmitt (9)	165
Brendan Frost (9)	166

Harlowbury Primary School, Old Harlow

Ewan Anthony Pinkett (8)	167
Taliah Rufuse (8)	168
Mia Brady (7)	169
Cherry Perez-Dusza (8)	170
Lacey Blackshaw (8)	171
Renee Firth-Moon (7)	172
Evie Beeson (8)	173
Faith Hinga (8)	174
Ella-Rose Jackson (8)	175

The Night

Every day is always a long day of school,
So I slouch onto my bed and wait for night to fall
I wait for my eyes to shut naturally,
Then the world turns into fantasy

When the clock strikes twelve, it is a stormy night
Then a wolf howls, which gives me a fright
Its tight overalls crease its shirt
The creature is probably hurt

It sacredly creates a galactic conspiracy,
What it's making looks like the galaxy
A cosmic glow beams through its heart
Is it healing its precious scars?

The astonishing thing turns into a galaxy,
The usual domestic world is no longer fantasy
I wake up and rise to my feet
I breathe quicker than a heartbeat

I bolt to the window and stare at the sky,
What I see gives me a sudden fright
It is the thing that the creature is holding in its hands
This makes me wet my pants.

Dawud Alshameri (11)

A Magical Place

When the sun goes down to rest and the moon lights up the dark night with its magical moonlight as bright as snow, everyone's dreams become either magical or dangerous, scary or weird, funny or sad, the night will make it happen and rest your eyes.
I am so excited to snuggle up in my bed with my softest blanket which keeps me warm and the little teddy that I hold tight as he cuddles me and will support me into my magical night. I'm waiting and waiting for my dream to come and make me happy or scared or sad.
Where will my imagination take me this time? Will it be as happy as chocolate? Will it be as funny as a green chicken? Or as scary as a ghost eating my candy? Nobody knows, but I now feel I'm falling quickly asleep.

The Dream:
I opened my eyes, it was morning already. I guess my dream had faded away leaving me like an empty memory box. Everything around me was kind of sad. You just asked me how do I know?
Well, my shoes started to cry when I put them on walking out of my bedroom, when I opened the door I was as tiny as an ant! The candy box was now so much higher than before. I was so disappointed but that wasn't all. I kept on walking towards the bathroom's door which was actually higher and away from me.

I tried to jump, to scream, to knock and bang, pretend to cry and also pretend to be the key going into the keyhole, but no use at all. "I wish I could be at least that high to reach the door's handle," I sighed. Then I said to myself, "I wish it is just a dream..."
Suddenly, as one of my tears dropped on the floor, I grew up tall again and I could finally reach the door's handle. Slowly I opened the door and entered the bathroom, where I saw another medium-sized door with the most beautiful colourful patterns that I'd ever seen. I opened that door and saw a tunnel which was coloured in purple and pink, with flowers around that started to dance and sprayed rainbow powder on me as I walked in.
Gently, I crept through the emerald-green long leaves, and as I did that I saw a wonderful garden with bright and giggling butterflies. A fountain was there with its water as blue as the sea, falling down in a magical crystal-clear lake.
The grass was filled with pretty cute flowers all dressed so nice and fancy. The fairies were dressed as rainbow butterflies, the princesses had the most elegant gowns walking gracefully on the meadow with flowers but not to hurt them, and the mermaids were swimming joyfully in the magical lake. When they lifted up their fins, a bright colourful rainbow pattern sparkled in the golden sun.

This place was so pretty, so magical and I didn't want to get out of it. When I looked at my pyjamas, they were gone and replaced with the most beautiful, colourful and bright long emerald dress that I had ever seen. My dress was actually made of pure emeralds and diamonds, the shoes were made of rainbow blossoms, and I was wearing a purple princess crown with stars shining so bright. I really felt like a princess. I was walking on an endless rainbow rising from the lake. I walked and walked, it felt so soft, it felt so good and I kept on walking.

I gently opened my eyes, it was morning again and the sun was awake. I remember and think about the beautiful dream that I just had. Such amazing things I saw in that dream, I will never forget it.

Nicole Carmen Stoicescu (10)

My Wizardly Life

Cauldron, wand, robe, book, owl, Patronus
I had it all
The first in the family, the first wizard born
I had no care, for my parents were Muggles
I got into Hogwarts, I got into Gryffindor
It was nervewracking, it was heart-stopping
But here I would learn the art of my power
Learn and be safe until the cursed one
Even came to this place
Of course, no one would dare
to even say his name
For he drank the blood of a unicorn
Cursed he was, everyone knew that
I'd fly on a broom
No worries, nor cares
I'd magic up my money
and shop in Diagon Alley
I'd never have to go to a shopping alley.

My life was good, even the best
The fun would never rest
I'd fly to the mountains
Dive in the sea
For I'd be living the life of luxury.

Maryam Rafi

Persistent Princess

Once upon a time, there lived a world called Dreamland. This planet made all the impossible dreams become possible by one single wish.
Just like the earth, Dreamland had a royal family called the Dolkaine. One special girl called Princess Maryam lived within this family, she had wavy black hair and loved the colour pink. Maryam was a humble child and helped everyone with her creative mind. All her guards were unicorns and wherever she went, the protectors followed.
One night, she planned to escape the palace and explore the outside world,
When midnight struck, the princess took one of her unicorns and flew out of the castle walls! Little did she know that once she left the palace her identity would vanish.
When Maryam was born, it was promised that not one person outside the palace walls would have any knowledge of a princess being born!
Dawn started to come close and the princess was so sleepy that her eyes couldn't stay open for more than ten seconds. She felt herself fading away and within a few moments, she fell on a few clouds and *bam!* She was consumed by the darkness... Now not one royal member ever left the castle because no good power was alive outside the walls. That one thing was never told to the princess which now caused a problem as Maryam was drifting into the evil monarchy!

She opened her eyes and her vision was red, she rubbed her eyes over and over again but still no change. Her hair was long and white, her skin had black butterflies moving towards her face, she screamed in disbelief and looked around for a mirror. She looked... different, older, and that's when she realised her necklace. A silver lining and the name 'Precisa' engraved with silver diamonds on top.
She turned around and saw the handle turning in the most peculiar way...

Maryam Khanom (8)

The Beautiful Earth

How beautiful, how beautiful this loving world can be,
And it is such an honour to inhabit it, you and me.
It makes me dizzy with wonder to stare at a vast blue sky,
Where the sun is grinning above our heads up high.

In a dream I had, barely days ago,
Emerald-green grass waved at me from below.
I was fizzing jubilant joy, like a glass of lemonade,
As I swayed to the bluebird's tune, I trusted every green blade.

Raindrops quenched the thirst of the ground, a cool, refreshing spray,
Then a rainbow shone around and brightened up my day.
All my worries forgotten, I was a cheery balloon,
As my heart felt warmer than fire, my soul leapt over the moon.

But then it all changed, my beaming bubble burst,
And as my sorrow cloaked me, I began to see the worst.
I felt isolated, alone, as scurrying squirrels made a dash,
And I felt my melody desert me, as grass turned to ash.

"Tell me what is happening!" I begged the phantom of fear,
And slowly, gradually, the truth started to draw near.
Did humans destroy the Earth on which birds once sang, elated?
The barren stretch of nothing on which I had waited.

On this cracked, sun-cooked flatbread which was like a dull jigsaw,
There were cracks that broke my heart and signs of life were no more.
Not a soul, not a beetle, lived in this terrible Earth,
Then I collapsed into a bundle and cried for all I was worth.

When I awoke, my eyes were sombre and grieving,
But I knew I must go on believing.

Our climate, precious climate, is changing,
And we're not listening, not engaging.
If we want to keep our beautiful Earth,
We need to act and give it new birth.

Holly Dimery (11)

The Forest Of Nightmares

As darkness swallowed the light
The city remained tranquil
I shut my eyes and entered a new world
A world I was going to regret visiting...
I could feel the trees gnarling at me
Their brown, rusty branches twining
How terrifying! What would I do?
The feeling of me being trapped like a prisoner in shackles
My heart began to pound with fright
All alone, I lay down
Then I began to remember
If this was a dream then I had to be somewhere but where was I?
Oh no, oh no! It was the Forest of Nightmares
It is said that if you go in, the only way out is death
The haunted forest, the most horrifying tunes were sung
Hoots and whispers in the darkness
Eyes lurking, many moves emerged from behind bushes
Hunting, waiting, beasts hiding, crouching in the shadows
The sky cackled, birds flew through
A river of red, flaming blood was filled

No sunlight shone through the piercing darkness
The forest, a beauty of nature but not what it seemed to be
Victims entered the gloom, wishing it was all a dream
Pure horror of lost souls remained uncovered
Scariest forms of the woodlands appeared
Paved into darkness, the dead-end route
Ultimate terror without a doubt
With nothing but murk, bodies lay all around
I woke up again
The soft feeling of my pillow
But wait... Why was there sweat all over it?
Then I thought and remembered what had happened
My mum came in to say, "Good morning, sweetie!"
I paused and did not reply
A flashback of my dream replayed in my head
Suddenly, I noticed that on my bedroom wall three words were written
Saying: 'You Are Next!'
Wait a moment... Was this thing referring to me?
"Oh yes I am!" it replied
I thought dreams would always be dreams
But you never know, they may come true...
Especially nightmares.

Eunice Opemipo Olagbolabo (10)

Panic Attack Strike

Running, running as fast as my legs would allow,
Keeping in mind the saying,
"Here comes the Boogie Man!"
Just the crazy thought of it makes me scream
I hope, I hope this is just a stupid dream
The faster I run, the more I lose hope
I push myself to keep up with the rapid pace
But all I'm doing is slowing myself down
I feel as though I'm in a chase
Memories are flooding me just like that,
Thoughts and thoughts of that neglected wooden bat
All of a sudden I feel a big stab in my heart,
I feel as though my entire body is being torn apart
I let my hand brush the ground,
But there's nothing to touch
My hands begin to feel numb
Don't know what to do,
Shouting, screaming, I finally realise,
No one can hear me
Falling, falling to the ground
The next thing I know,
I can feel my heart pounding out of my chest
I awake from this terrible nightmare
Covered in pure sweat and ringing in my ears

I have realised again
That it was all just fears
Pounding and pounding in my heart
Just won't stop
Faster and faster the beat goes
I feel like I'm on stage talking on a microphone,
I wonder why I'm feeling like this in my cosy little shack,
Then I finally realise it was just a panic attack.

Aqsa Ali

Nothing Will Be The Same Anymore

Nothing will be the same anymore
Today is my first day of secondary school
Doesn't that sound really cool?
But there's an alarm bell ringing inside my head,
Can't I just stay at home instead?
I gulp down my breakfast as quick as a flash,
My mind is racing and all my thoughts are trash.
Nothing will be the same anymore.
The gates open like my mind,
Ready for my new school as I leave mine behind.
The leaves usher me inside the gates,
Then I see people hanging out with their mates.
What if I make no friends?
This is so different from my old school.
Nothing will be the same anymore.
All the lessons are a drag,
I don't know why I packed so much stuff in my bag.
Now it is break time and I have nobody to play with,
I feel isolated and really scared,
There are all these negative thoughts nagging about in my head.
Nothing will be the same anymore.

But wait, what's that sound?
I can hear it all around.
Oh no, is it the fire alarm?
Wait a minute...
It sounds like my alarm clock!
But then I wake up and realise it was just a dream,
I can feel a shiver down my spine.
But one thing's for sure,
Nothing will be the same anymore.

Breanna Obeng (11)

My Living Classroom

Last night I saw my classroom laughing,
Rulers got the giggles
And worksheets completely creased themselves!
Dorky dictionaries chuckled foolishly,
Whilst pencils laughed hysterically!
Whiteboards were funnily lying on the ground
And tearing up with laughter!

Last night I saw my classroom dancing,
Pencils leapt gracefully from table to table,
Like an adorable, cute bunny
Sand timers were wiggling their hips
And leading a stationery parade!
Rubbish bins were grooving along to music
While recklessly spilling trash!

Last night I saw my classroom crying,
Blunt pencils felt useless and alone,
As they watched sharpeners break effortlessly
Computers threw a technical tantrum
Whilst getting attacked by viruses!

Last night I saw my classroom fighting
Black pens were maliciously spraying ink on paper
Whilst pencils were wildly stripping off their shavings!

Terrible trays hurled at furious pots
Like a livid monster terrorising a city
Water bottles became so furious,
They flooded the entire classroom!

Jaimee Luspo (10)

The Climate Didn't Change

Once upon a dream, the climate didn't change,
The world finally did feel very strange
I am too dumb to dream, as not all of us are on the same page
I dreamt about climate change

I dreamt about having a green and healthy world,
And not having an Earth like the Underworld
The dark side of the Earth finally turned
I dreamt about climate change

I dreamt about the slightest change,
Of not having pollution
This is indeed like having a diamond chain
I dreamt about climate change

The number of organisms finally increased,
The gas finally didn't get released
My sadness finally decreased
I dreamt about climate change

Living things lived a longer life
I finally enjoyed looking at the wildlife
It was like being healed by being stabbed by a knife
I dreamt about climate change

My dream was to save the Earth,
To me, it felt like a second birth
My dream was to save the Earth

I dreamt about climate change
I dreamt about having a healthy Earth
I dreamt about climate change.

Abishan Jesuthas

Once Upon A Dream

I dream of a land far away,
Where you can play all day
It becomes a circus at night
Clowns wake you up with quite a fright.

Unicorns prance,
And giraffes dance
Princesses declare,
Which is pretty unfair.

You could have a school where teachers are nice,
Always having a choice of turning them into mice
At least they get you somewhere in life,
Maybe you will have a wife.

Time stands still,
Never getting ill
Never getting old,
Not even bald.

Never having to worry,
Get a McDonald's McFlurry!
Learn to ride a train,
Or even meet Harry Kane.

See the trees blossom,
Or even meet a possum
Decide what you want to be when you grow up,
You could groom a snow pup.

Listen to your favourite singers,
You could be mingers
Smell the flowers,
They will give you special powers.

Not to brag but my dream is the best,
Put it to the test
It will pass,
As easy as you can break glass.

Megan Rosemary Neale (10)

A River's Journey

One cold and wet day
I saw a river passing my way,
It had waves like splashing lava
But I started to think I'd rather,
Be floating on that river in a golden boat
And then started to think I should play a note,
The river would be floating in the breeze
As I start to pass many trees

Suddenly I went into the dark part of the jungle,
And then I heard something starting to rumble
Out of the jungle came a big hippo
As he jumped into the water,
Like a speeding limo
He splashed me with water,
Maybe about a quarter

When the hippo went away,
The river was nice and calm
Nothing to be near me
Nothing to harm,
When I opened my eyes again
I was back in my bedroom,
Still gazing out at the sleeping town
I also thought I could see my golden boat

Saying goodbye now,
Just as I was about to go to sleep,
In the distance, I could see
The river splitting out into the ocean
And my golden boat with it too.

Savannah Williston (7)

Was It A Dream?

On one snowy night, I lay in my bed
I closed my eyes, almost thinking I was dead
I yawned for one last time
Then darkness fell upon my tired, heavy eyes

Next thing I knew, I was soaring through the sky
Like a bird so high, enjoying its life
I flew through white, fluffy clouds and mountains and rivers
Little did I know that soon would differ
Crash!

What had happened?
Where was I now?
"Are you okay?" a soft voice exclaimed
I looked up to see pure beauty
Her eyes were aqua-blue
Blonde hair cascaded down her back
A red silk dress covered her body
Fangs like knives glinted in the moonlight
"Vampire!" I shouted
I turned, skimming the fangs from piercing my neck
But it was too late, I had been bitten

I opened my eyes, gasping for air
"It's okay, kiddo, just a bad dream!" Mum exclaimed
My neck absorbed a sharp pain
Blood trickled down my neck
Had it been a dream?

Jack William Machin (10)

My Dream

In this dreamland lies the sapphire ground,
A carpet of white and blue.
Birds soar making a melodious sound,
Spreading in the air like the flu.

The sky appears an emerald-green,
Still spreading a lush carpet of life.
Occasionally, white rubs the green clean,
A solution clearing strife.

Mystical creatures wander and roam,
Flapping their elegant wings.
Their powerful horns place magic in their home,
These creatures are bright and beautiful things.

Despite all these special sights,
There are bad parts too.
Darkness lies behind bright lights,
Now let us hear one or two:

Bang! Eruptions fall from the sky,
Cannons of fire stain the clouds.
The sound as it falls is a battle cry,
But also is harmless to crowds.

Far away toxic gas drifts,
In this area, you must *gulp!* for air.
Luckily though, it lies far but it shifts,
But with the creature's spells, it can't compare.

To this dreamland, we must bid our farewells,
Until I slumber once more.
In this world full of spells,
What wonders will it have in store...?

Tvisha Lakshmeesh

Slumber

My tired eyes fall into a deep sleep,
No need today to count sheep
Nothing can wake my slumber
I enter my world with thunder

My sky bright, shining yellow,
Like a star twinkling as I mellow
The birds are tweeting my favourite song,
This is my world, we all sing along

Superheroes are busy saving the planet
And the Lego people are building with a mallet
The trees grow money,
And the seas are full of honey

I float in the clouds
As down below it gets loud
I am free to follow my destiny to the end
To help those in need to heal and mend
Unicorns exist...
The Earth is just a mist

The school here is nice and cheerful
No bullies here so can't be fearful
Everyone is free to think and see
Being happy and respectful is the key

This is my world which exists in space,
Nothing is different, no disability or race
Everyone is accepted for who they are
We work together so we can go far.

Ayaan Saqib (9)

Once Upon A Dream

Once upon a dream,
I thought that I could be
A dragon flying through the sky
A knight in shining armour
And a superhero who could never die
Or a president like Obama!

Once upon a dream,
I thought that I could see
A twisting golden yellow road,
A mystical magic wand
As well as myself kissing a little
Green, tiny toad
And a console with games connected to the TV!

Once upon a dream,
I believed it could really be
That I kissed a beautiful damsel
And married her easily
I felt like all the wishes
Weren't actually burning
Like they were in reality!

Once upon a dream,
I saw it scarily
Myself as an old person
That hung on very dearly
I'd written a few old books
And I'd lost all fairy dreams
As well as the shining armour
Plus, I never was Obama
Why, oh dearie me!

And once upon a dream...
I was resting as well as can be!

Ayomide David Ajayi (10)

Candy Shop

According to the rumours I've heard,
A secret candy shop is hidden in town
It is somewhere very absurd
In the place you least expect

The shop is vibrant and beautiful,
It is really unique
The sweets are mouth-watering and colourful,
The shop has every chocolate and candy you'd ever imagine

Inside, you can pick and choose the sweet you'd like to buy
After you eat it, something weird will happen
The sweets will give you a power,
It has been said superheroes were created this way

The candy shop is owned by a woman who wears a mask,
Her face is never revealed
She doesn't speak and lives alone
Well, that is what it seems, you wouldn't dare ask

According to the rumours I've heard,
A secret candy shop is hidden in town

It might be true or even fantasy
The candy shop is a mystery yet to be discovered.

Haniya Hanif (11)

Revenge Of The River

Pamba was an elegant river,
Many people lived on the riverbanks
It had many vibrant fish and millions of plants,
It had trees surrounding it.

The prettiest was pebbles,
In monsoon season, the river overflows and children come to play and fish
The pebbles and raindrops were very good friends,
So the raindrops looked forward to monsoon season.

Once when they came, the pebbles weren't there,
The river lost its beauty,
The raindrops got sad
They searched the river upside down,
So it came back as wind and rain.

There they were,
Stuck onto a palace,
So the raindrops went and came back stronger.

As days went by, the rain became a flood,
It went higher and higher until it reached the pebbles
When they saw each other,
They hugged and talked,
But then they had to say bye.

The raindrop said,
"I'll come again stronger than ever and take you back!"

So the pebbles became happy,
And they are still waiting.

Rithika Raghunandanan (7)

Titanic: A Ship's Journey

She was white, black, red and gold
A beautiful ship she was, so bold
With her walls a colourful charade
It was like an indoor parade

Now she was ready for her trip
Into the water for a dip
And then off she'd sail
With all of her royal mail

All the passengers were very impressed,
That the crew had done their very best
With all the luxury food
The passengers were certainly in the mood

But suddenly, during the night,
Captain Smith got a fright
The ship skidded against the ice
Passengers in hysterics for paying the price

Everyone was screaming very loud,
And Captain Smith was not proud
She was halved into two ships,
To know she couldn't go on any more trips

Now she is the bottom of the sea
And this is where she will always be
Sitting silently down
And she is still there now.

Kaitlyn Weir (10)

Harry's Dreams

At night there are so many thoughts
That whirr inside my brain
Some pop up for the first time
Some time and time again

Family, friends, computer games
All kinds of things
Holidays and swimming pools
And riding my bike!

How do these thoughts get into my head,
And why? I'd like to know
How do they end up in my bed,
Through sunshine, rain or snow?

When Mum says, "Lights out, time for sleep!"
My dreams say, "Here we go!"
"Homework, school and aeroplanes,
Goomba, Bowser and Mario!"

My world of dreams is magic,
Exciting, thrilling and fast
I can't predict where they'll take me
Or how long they're going to last...

If by chance, I might get scared
I'm very, very glad
I'll jump out of my own bed
And in with Mum and Dad.

Harry Cheesman (7)

Imagine That

I have a dream,
To have a factory full of chocolate,
Chocolate like a melting snowflake,
Oreo-like melting icicles,
Also, caramel like melting honey

I have a dream,
To have furniture,
A couch as comfy as a spa
A TV as interesting as a detector,
A bed to dream on like a hero,
A cupboard to dress like royalty,
A bath to have a nice bath and relax

I have a dream,
To travel around the world,
Antarctica as cold as an iceberg,
Egypt as hot as the oven,
Italy has a tasty pizza as juicy as a mango,
Nigeria has Jollof as spicy as a pepper,
Turkey has turkey as big as a chicken

I have a dream,
To dream big,
I will dream big by,

Going to a chocolate factory,
To taste like a professional,
To eat like a king,
I will dream big by,
Sleeping on a bed to dream big,
And having a good time,
I will dream big by,
Travelling all around the world,
Having a fun time,
And having a dream.

Temiloluwa Emmanuel Kalejaiye (9)

Meat World

Oh, when I visited Meat World,
The swimming pool was gravy!
I decided to take a closer look,
And to my surprise, I saw a little chicken drumstick that looked like a baby.

When I visited Meat World,
The steaks were running around like mad!
I think it was hard to control them,
Because they were with their lazy old grandad.

Oh, when I visited Meat World,
There was a herd of bacon and lamb.
All shouting for desperate help, for they were getting picked up,
By the meat world's giant, to go into the oven and pan.

When I visited Meat World,
Oh, the smell was mouth-watering,
I ran to my destiny.
I couldn't resist it any longer!
But before I knew it, the meat world giant liked slaughtering things,
So I gave them to him instead.

Catriona MacKinnon

Once Upon A Nightmare

An eerie echo circled my breath,
Darkness lay upon my thoughts
A rush of dread pounded through my heart
I was hit by a tornado of emotions
A foul odour, so strong
Blocked the perfume I was wearing

I heard scuttles from whatever lay beneath the depths of this cave,
Movement caught my eye
I squinted at the damp ground
Nothing,
Nothing was there

With a flash of burning light,
The sky illuminated
Recklessly, I stepped forward,
Closer to the abnormal mysteries awaiting my arrival
Cold daggers ran down my spine

A slimy texture crawled down my skin
As I acknowledged the gust of wind
Pulling my hairs upwards,
Endlessly, the painful sound of water dripping raced through my mind.

Kaitlin Elizabeth Grafton (11)

Once Upon A Dream

I once was so little
So pretty and fleek
And I went on a mission,
A mission, that's it

I wanted to find it,
To find the great kit
The kit of survival
Survival, that's it

The days were so long,
And the nights were so cold
I wanted my mummy
My mummy, that's it

I stayed on my own
Until I found something thick
I went to go check it
To check it, that's it

I saw it,
And pulled it
And took it
Until

I had seen it
I had found it
I'd found it, that's it

I was so happy,
To find the great kit
The kit of survival
Survival, that's it

I took it away,
And made my way home,
And I was so happy
I'd found it, that's it.

Chanelle Gatheru (11)

Once Upon A Dream

Once upon a dream, there was a boy called Josh.
He was fast and he was furious,
He was sporty and curious.

Once upon a dream, he became a child football star.
His shirt was forty-four,
In fact, that's all he ever wore.

Once upon a dream, he was spotted by a scout.
He would practise every day,
He was desperate to play.

Once upon a dream, he walked out onto the pitch.
His strip was all fitted,
He was totally committed.

Once upon a dream, he won the World Cup for Belgium.
He ran faster than a car,
On that day, he was the star.

Once upon a dream, he would inspire others to play.
He taught his kids all the skills,
On the terrace, they did their drills.

Once upon a time, it finally came true...
He was the star of the winning team,
It wasn't just a dream!

Joshua Nahmad

When I'm Older

When I'm older,
I want to be
A teacher
So that is what I will be
I want to educate children
Teach them all they need
Maths, English, science
And of course, how to read.

When I'm older,
I want to be
A care worker
So that is what I will be
I want to look after kids in care
By being friendly and kind
Show them they are amazing
When they put it to their mind.

When I'm older,
I want to be
Someone who works with animals
So that is what I will be
I don't mind what type of animals I work with
As long as they can see

That not everyone is loud and pushy
That some can be like me.

When I'm older,
I want to be
Someone who makes a difference
So that is what I will be
When I'm older
I want to be
Someone inspirational
As well as just being me!

Poppy Alice Smeeton

My Dreamy Bunk Bed

My dreamy bunk bed is the bed I rest my sleepy head
My dreamy bunk bed helps me plan things I do,
Like this poem I'm writing to you!
My dreamy bunk bed helps me to have wonderful dreams
Like... I've dreamt
I was a scientist (which is one of the things I'd like to be)
I'd study how many neurons are in an animal's brain,
And work out why people have pain.
I've dreamt to be an architect who'd build big and small,
I'd build a building greater than the China wall.
I've dreamt to be an inventor who'd invent great and small,
I'd probably invent a cleaning machine three metres tall.
I've dreamt to be a doctor who'd help young and old,
Not just to get better, but to be strong and bold.

Fara Adesakin (8)

Close Your Eyes And Listen

Close your eyes and listen,
To the flowing of the stream
Like a river of sparkling crystals
It's like living in a breathtaking dream

Close your eyes and listen,
To the crashing of the thunder
Like the roar of a majestic lion
Its unsteady rhythm makes you wonder

Close your eyes and listen,
To the gurgle of the frogs
Like a chorus of magnificent opera singers
They chant upon their logs

Close your eyes and listen,
To the curtain of the rain
Like a steady downpour of tears
It hammers the rainforest in pain

Close your eyes and listen
To each wonderous sound
Like orchestras playing
There's music all around.

Tayla Brady (10)

William The Wicked Wolf

William has greasy, matted brown fur
Horrible hypnotising eyes
Dagger-like yellow teeth
Claws as sharp as horns

One dark day an evil plan came into his brain
He thought his plan was genius
He would need an army to help him
He would go to the village

The nice people took one look at him and fainted with shock
When they woke, they saw his horrible hypnotic eyes staring into theirs
They were hypnotised
He had lots of evil servants to help him to defeat the worst enemy of his life

With his evil gang, he went to war with Wally the Woodcutter
Wally was an utter nutter
William and his gang tried to defeat him
But it was no use
They lost
The spell was broken

William the wicked wolf was no more
He was never seen again.

Katie Thornton (6)

Planet Love!

Climate change is bad,
It makes the planet sad
The Earth's temperature is rising,
And our polar bears are crying

We need to control our daily habits,
Because someday, every living thing
Will die
Even rabbits!

Already, the grounds are cracking
And water is lacking
We need to help the world,
We need to help the sea
And we need to make the air that we breathe
Go clean

So come on and save our world,
By stopping coal and fuels being burnt
And don't be lazy
Because that drives me crazy!
Oh my gosh!
The planet is getting hotter,
So *please* start recycling,
Like your neighbour, Mr Potter.

Emily Agha Mohammad Zadeh (10)

Dream The Stars

As my dream awoke from its display...
I reached for the star.
And held it in my hand.
In a snowy mystical sunset.
In a visit to another land.
With emerald evergreen trees,
And crystal-clear pearl slopes,
And exquisite, enchanting, snow-capped summits.
This was all I had ever hoped.
Lethal black-as-midnight horses stampeded in the path
While red deer strode through the slippery slopes
In a luxury picturesque cabin in Germany,
We were eating gooey-licious melted marshmallows,
Drinking hot cocoa by the campfire.
As the snow strode.
Bang!
Then the cascading hostile avalanche awoke from its slumber...
I reached for the star,
And I was in my bed.
I reached for the star,
And I was exactly where I said.

Victoria Mmesoma Nwachukwu (10)

The Quadria

As I get thrown into the room,
I struggle to see through the gloom
The room is dark, drenched in misery
There are four wooden doors standing tall in front of me

Which one should I choose? I cannot decide,
I feel so apprehensive about what lies inside
Slowly, I step towards door number three,
It's like a magnet, uncontrollably pulling me

As I anxiously reach for the handle,
The door begins to creak
It slowly starts to open,
As I try to take a peek

I'm faced with a wonderland covered in snow,
The white winter glistens
With a mysterious glow
I cautiously head out to have fun and explore...

Sophie Gelder (10)

Once Upon A Dream

O ne night I fell asleep
N ever a bad dream, they're not a treat
C an't wait for my next wonderful adventure
E ver so dreamy and ever so sweet

U p high on the treetops
P etals fell on me
O n my way to Fairyland
N ever a dull moment, you'll see

A shining star glowed in the night

D ancing and prancing, it's such a sight
R ound the tree and to the end
E ver so fun and a letter I'll send
A m I going to see Fairyland again?
M aybe, we'll see as long as it doesn't rain.

Abby-Lee Cliffe

The Candy Bar Galaxy

A swirly pink lolly appears in the distance,
To the other planets as small as an ant.
A constellation is formed every way,
To be the best of every man's day.

M&M's were encrusted with a pearly white,
It was so sweet you could take a bite.
Twix's caramel is really hidden,
To eat is forbidden.

Jelly babies cry,
So nice you could have a try.
Mars has a black wrapper,
And a good rapper.

Maltesers have intimidating teasers,
But they have good teachers
Kit and Kat are twin planets,
Both creators of milky nets.

Chewit has a peculiar history,
And will remain a mystery.
Toffee is very chewy,
Its layer is very gooey.

Oluwatamilore Gabriel Kalejaiye (10)

Way Of The Dragon

Up the mountain in a mythical cave
A dragon lived that was terrifying and fearsome
Casting fear over the kingdom

The king sent thousands of men
Even the strongest warriors
But not one survived

Its fire-breathing mouth is an artwork by Picasso
Red, fiery eyes glared down at the knights
With green, slimy scales as hard as rocks
Menacing tail whipped knights off castle turrets

Wings so powerful
Only a magic sword could slay it
Its quick reaction from turn to turn
He is the king of the skies!

Have you ever imagined an awesome sight?

Ray Marcou (10)

Candy Express

Minty green mountains
In the faraway distance
Tasty chocolate chip ice cream disappearing
As I munch away
As I walk on the scrumptious rainbow Skittle path
It crunches like rocks being cracked
As soon as I get into a giant banana split boat,
The sweet temptation is too high
So I definitely can't resist gobbling up the delicious banana split boat
Delicious pink candyfloss clouds gracefully float in the teal-blue sky
Chocolate chip cookies make my mouth water with greed
Chocolate trees make me faint because I love them so much
On the Candy Express.

Lexie Elina Sabatelli (9)

Once Upon A Dream

After kissing Mum goodnight,
I travelled to the land of dreams
The moon sends rays of light
And the sun sends happy beams.

I chose a comet as my carriage,
And it was going very fast
I had a race with aliens,
And I never ever came last.

I landed on a moon,
And planted a flag
I met some alien friends,
Who wanted to play a tag.

They wanted to take me to another planet
But it was too far
Instead, I said I'd take them to Earth,
Travelling together on a shooting star.

Suddenly I heard an alarm clock,
I came out of my dream
I wish it would have been real,
But in the future it will it seems.

Anoushka Apte (10)

Happiness

I woke up
On the hard, wet grass
The rain
Covered my body

It was all grey
It had always been that way
Until I saw this man
He was the one who changed everything

I grabbed his weird-looking hand
While he led the way
Will this
Be my happiness today?

A rainbow was there in front of me
He led me to happiness
My only dream
Was to see a colour

He dragged my body
As I threw myself on the rainbow carpet
And we flew through the land,
Passing all the markets

They offered us sweets, cake extra
But I'd kindly passed

My eyes could not believe a thing...

But,
I woke up from that dream.

Princess Ahmed

Diego Garcia, My Paradise

My paradise in the Indian Ocean,
Diego Garcia, where tall coconut palms dominate and surround
Eastpoint plantation.
Kids running,
Kids shouting,
Kids skipping,
Kids fishing
Strong men, deshelling coconuts.
Sweating, but will finish their tasks.
Drinking water from coconuts
and eating its flesh, to gain more strength.
Women working in the Corpa factory area, singing
"Diego Garcia, Diego Garcia, my only place, my paradise."
Diego Garcia, my beautiful dream.
Soon I woke up, but it was nowhere to be seen.

Allena Vincatassin (10)

Once Upon A Dream

O ver the hilltops
N ever under a tree
C an you see a wonderful dream?
E nd all the nightmares, please. Do this for me

U pon a star
P leading for an amazing dream
O n an adventure
N ever to be seen

A nd don't let the adventure fly away

D reams, dreams always remain
R emember, have fun
E xciting things can happen to anyone
A lways remember the shooting star
M any people have dreams too so remember this conversation between you and me. Catching dreams isn't easy, can't you see?

Izabel Cliffe

Once Upon A Dream...

I was in Mumbles, yes, a peculiar name,
But maybe, just maybe, it will roar in fame!
'The Best Holiday Place' trophy, you claim,
Mumbles wouldn't be the same.

On the beach, sheathed in sand,
Hearing the music from the band
The sea as fierce as ever before, swept my feet on the land,
Oh, I loved it, how grand!

Next, fresh fried fabulous fish,
Of course on the dish
Oh very yummy, my teeth going mish-mash-mish!
Lemonade on the house, delish!

Oh, the lovely vivid view,
On the leaves the droplets of dew
The sky, the sea mainly blue,
All too good to be true!

Jack Hei Lee (10)

One Night

Once upon a dream,
In a magical land
I saw a penguin eating cream
And a unicorn in glittery sand.

I was riding a horse
With a tail of gold.
It could be worse
I could become old
Or the horse could be bald.

All the doughnuts were floating around.
The chocolate fountain was hitting the ground.
The marshmallow mountain reached the sky,
I wanted to fly.

It was lots of fun,
I woke to the sun.
I climbed out of bed and fell on my head
The day had begun, my dream was done.

Alexandra Rosemary Isabella Woods

Once Upon A Dream

Once upon a dream
I was so tired,
I wanted to scream

The night was magical and dark
I dreamt of playing
In the sunny park

I used a swing to reach the blue sky,
I hopped on the cloud and went up high

I saw a beautiful beach
I had golden warm sand
All over my little feet

Hidden in the sand,
I found some big shells
I listened to one of them
And heard ringing bells

I woke up in my warm cosy bed
I told my mum all about
The once upon a dream I had.

Mya (7)

Dream

Today is the day,
Tonight is the night,
Dream in full colour,
Stand in the spotlight.

Through nightmares;
Fire, water, storms and lightning
Crackling, striking the roofs of great buildings,
Tears streaming from a face you know,
Dripping down the drains far below.

Happy outbursts lift your heart;
Sun shining bright,
Reach for the light,
Set up and fly a kite,
Let it lift you up to the highest height.

Through the dreams you encounter,
Take the opportunities you have,
Live in a castle, climb up a tower,
Take every one of the opportunities you have.

Connor Sado (11)

Deep Dreams

Shimmering,
In sapphire-blue waters
A fish lay sleeping underneath the waves,
While people up top went skimming for days.

On the other side of the water,
No one knows what lies.
Just the fish that sits and waits for a surprise.

Some people go fishing just to test which fish is the best.
But some are glorious in their quest,
And come home triumphant with fish for every mouth.
But still do not know how magical the diamond-coloured water is
With its magnificent waves.

The brave silverfish,
That still sleep
Know,
And keep their secret
Carefully.

William John Henry Reavill (9)

Once Upon A Dream

I went to a secret chocolate door,
With a shiny chocolate floor
I saw all the delicious chocolates
I wish I could touch and taste
But the fairy came and
Took me to Gummy Bear Land
I saw a giant gumball machine
With colourful gummies
Suddenly a big gummy bear came
With gummy cake that tasted so yummy
And said,
"Happy birthday, Khadija!"
Everyone ate the rainbow cake and sang,
"This is Gummy Bear Land
Happy birthday, Khadija,
Happy birthday, Khadija!"

Khadija Saleh

Tail

A fashion designer, that's my dream
I sail across the sea to be what I want to be
I swim underwater to my shop
This won't be a flop!

A lovely mermaid waiting for me
Deep down in the sea
I tell her to put her tail forward
I take out my mermaid's tools
I'm no fool!

When I'm done
Everyone stares
They all stay it's not fair
They say, "Where did you get your tail from?"
And she says, "That shop down there."

Hajra Jamshed (10)

Hedgehogs

H appy, harmless creatures wandering through the woods
E veryone needs to save hedgehogs
D id you know they curl up into a ball for sleep and defence?
G ather around to save these poor hogs
E ven though they've been around for thousands of years
H elp them survive for thousands more
O ur prickly friends need your help
G ardens can be dangerous places
S o make sure your gardens are hedgehog friendly and tell others to as well!

Lachlan Lasikiewicz (10)

A Nightmare I Won't Forget

Tonight, I go to sleep,
I dream of a dream...
Dark and deep

I see things very strange,
Like steps so very steep

I walk,
I take a step,
I hear someone talk

A whisper behind me,
No, below me!
This creep stalks!
It screams and shouts!
Curses and offensive language,
That gives me doubts!

It creeps towards me...
I feel like I'm in Scouts!
It leaps towards me...
Bang!

"Am I free?
Am I safe?"
My mum is on her knee,

Looking at me,
"You're safe... for now."

Haniyah Iman Yaqub (10)

The Night Sky

All the stars are bright
Shining in the night
Make a wish tonight

The sky is black
Shine everywhere
To brighten up the sky

Stars with shining light
Guide our way tonight
Make it clear and bright

Brighten up the last of our day
Shine so fine
Make this place better all through the night

Grant our wishes
Shine so clear
Will you show us the way?

For skies are black
In midnight
Please guide us every night.

Ellie Wong (8)

My Fairyland Adventure

My Fairyland adventure started one day,
Me and the fairies loved to play
In our house, we saw a little mouse
Running along, singing a song
He saw a little bunny, he thought it was funny
They went off together and ate some honey
The bunny thought it was funny
To see the mouse eating honey
It went down to his tummy
Bunny and Mouse sat on a stool
Watching fairies in the pool
Some of the fairies thought it was cool
To see a bunny and a mouse sitting on a stool.

Amber Clements

Candyland

Candyland is the place that I love to go,
Candyland is the place where you can't grow!
Candyland is the place that you can have fun,
But after this visit, you might weigh a ton!
The reason for this is because,
The trees are made of candyfloss!
Growing on the candyfloss trees,
Are fruity jellies shaped like knees.
Every house has a roof of sweets,
And there are even lollipop seats!
The roads are embedded with chocolate rolls,
And there are even baby foals!
Would you like to visit Candyland?

Summer Samantha Green (10)

Without Wings

It was death-defying; it was scary; it was even hard to believe,
Me jumping off a skyscraper? Yes! I just said that indeed,
They shouted, "One, two, three!" and I let gravity do its thing,
I felt like a superhero but without the wings,
I plummeted headfirst, I thought I was the worst,
But realised my luck had changed, when out of the water I burst!
So listen, children, anything is possible, if imagined in your dreams,
You just have to unlock your mind and drift into the unseen.

Alisha Taylor (10)

The Day I Lost My Name

The teacher said to me,
"Mia, what is the answer?"
My brain was twisting around
Who could Mia be?
I just answered a random number
Who could I possibly be?
I was really puzzled,
Could I be a girl or boy?
Could I be good or bad?
My mind was absolutely baffled
Everyone looked at me as if I was a weirdo
Until five minutes later...

I hit my head on the table!
Now I remember who I am,
I am Mia!

Hirah Khan

Dreary Dream

Calm, peaceful, moonlit night
The sun says bye-bye,
And the stars say hi,
And shine bright.

Patter, patter!
"Aargh, spider!"
Marching proudly on the floor,
It crawled through the door.

Hang on!
What's it doing with the sharpener?
Freaks! Invader!

Scratch!

It made me full of heed,
When my finger began to bleed.

Never did I know,
That spiders were so clever,
So I'd rather tie my bow,
And stay away from them forever!

Oh, what a dreary dream...

Aish Sarmad

Sports On The Moon

On the moon, what could we do?
Play a friendly game of football?
We tried, but the ball went so quickly
Then we tried to ice skate
But it didn't really work
Do you want to know why?
The next thing we did was netball
Which was the same as football.

After these sports
The next one was lacrosse
When we passed the ball
It flew up so high
What could we do next?
Are there any more sports?
Who knows?

Daniel Martin Haynes (9)

Science

Like maths,
Photosynthesis, gas
Experiment, test
Try your best
Gravitational force, air resistance
Albert Einstein
Solid! Liquid!
Who knows what it's like,
In the world of technology?
World of robots
Who knows?
Your heart's beating
Louder and louder
Like a tiger roaring
Explosion!
Electricity, circuits
Wires, digital
In the world of...
Wireless, technology
Science!

Kamy Patel (10)

Swimming In Tea

I was swimming in tea,
My skin was all red,
It was like I was on fire,
I couldn't even go to bed,
I was swimming in tea,
Now I was extremely red,
I was like sizzling bacon,
I couldn't even feel my head,
I woke up the next morning in dread,
I drank some more tea,
Now I was really embarrassed,
But some people thought I was fine,
I poured water on myself,
Now I was better than ever!

Munashe Whitlam Mazenge (9)

Punch, Punch, Punch

I have a crunchy friend.
He feels like a root
Before peeling his skin.
He likes boxing and playing with me.
He comes from Carrot Land, in India.
He is very good for our eyes,
He is very rough.
He always wins in the boxing competition.
He teaches me and my friend,
When he comes to Gabon.
My best friend in the world,
When I sleep,
He comes into my dreams.
My best friend.

Harshita Srihari (7)

Unicorns

U nicorns are very, very pretty
N ever think you will never see a unicorn
I t is a magical world that does not exist
C andy always makes you feel in a better mood
O ut of this world, there is lots of rainbow-coloured candy
R ainbow colours are everywhere
N ever let your wishes go, they may come true
S ome are big, some are small, but they are magical.

Fiorella (7)

My Dream Of Being An Author

Oh how I would love to be an author
It's just so fun writing books
You can get famous
And be an amazing storyteller

All the things you can achieve
Books can teach kids
New things
And also stories

It's as fun as rolling down a roller coaster
And reading feels like an imaginary teacher
New things whoosh into your head
Oh how I would love to be an author.

Onur Hurriyetoglu (8)

Once Upon A Dream

O n fluff
N ear rainbows
C lear colours
E scaping into dreamland

U p on a plane
P alaces on the sun
O rdinary is different
N ormal but strange

A lways vivid

D rifting on clouds
R osy is amazing
E ven daydreams are sweet
A mazing is weird
M eant to be wild.

Sophia Wretham

My Nightmare

A nightmare everyone does have,
Fears as well, ruin your life they can
"Arghh!" normally happens
This is what scares me

   S adness, snakes and also socks
   C ountryside, do we have to give that house a knock?
   A trocious behaviour, of course you know!
   R ats who crawl all over you in your dreams
   Y ucky food, yes, I am also the same!

Teghvir Singh

A Writer's Dream

Some people,
Born with a pen in their hand
Stories carefully planned,
Rich description and detail.

Inspiration,
We provide,
As a simple guide,
Easy and well thought out.

Stories,
And poems are key
Sitting on our knee,
Writing our imagination on a piece of paper.

In writing,
A possibility
Shows your ability,
And how you think.

We will dream differently,
We are different
Because,
We are writers!

Naomi Lily Stanyer (11)

The Dreamscape

Slimy slugs and spiders too
Ghosts and ghouls in four, three, two...
Monsters wailing
Blobs flailing
An eerie feeling on your arm
A phantom horse from a phantom farm

You try to run but you can't get away,
You open your eyes and it's suddenly day
Oh, it was a nightmare, a weird one too
So you walk away but there's a drip of goo...

Muhammad-Abdisalam Ahmed

Mr Monkey Alien Hunt

Mr Monkey is on an alien hunt,
He is going to find a brave one
He's not scared,
Suddenly, out of the blue,
He sees a shadow
In the corner of the moon
Out from the crater
Jumps an alien alligator
Mr Monkey invites him for tea,
And says, "Come with me!"
They hop into the rocket,
Blast off and shout, "Whee!"

Mia Sahni (10)

The Guardian Of Life

In her eyes, the sun has she
Then for her dress, silky clouds, but the sleeves woven grass
In her rings water and sand, with a dash of pebbles
In her earrings, the moon
Her hair is lit by stars and has all our names embroidered on
And her glass high heels has she in
The leaves and bark of all vast trees
As for her heart, it is as pure as gold.

Lara Hardee Dorsett (8)

The Opposite Me

I wish there was a parallel universe,
Somewhere in the sky
The world could get even worse
If only I could fly

Another one of me,
Wouldn't that be cool?
Does it have a sea?
What about a school?

Some people have visions,
But nothing can be true
What about a universe collision?
Just think an opposite you!

Olivia Prendergast

Mr Dragon!

Where are you Mr Dragon?
When I ride on your back, I feel I am on the rainbow!
All your beautiful colours shine like stars in the night sky.
When you are high up, you look like a rainbow aeroplane over the horizon with the fluttering birds.
Now please come back, we can fly through the sky, make friends with the birds and even explore the country!

Ziyue Zhou (9)

Daydreams

D rift off
A way from reality
Y ummy ideas floating inside my head
D istant voices fading away
R unning away to another world
E ffortless beauty surrounds
A ll for me, a place of serenity
M oving slowly back to reality
S orrow, it's at an end.

Bethany Wretham

My World

In the real world, I always cry
Bullying and trouble
Always knocking at my door
So that's why I made a world
In my dreams
So I could escape
From all the sadness
That comes my way
But when my worries and fears got bigger and bigger
They got in
I ran and ran but could not escape,
That's why I never saw that world again.

Ayomide Deborah Aboyeji (10)

Ancient Abandoned Theme Park

Once upon a dream, there were two sisters
That adventured into an abandoned theme park and they thought:
Rusty oil surrounded the rides
As they looked around, they had no pride
As they stared at a fence, it was all burnt
When they tried to look for happiness
They knew what they had learnt.

Chloe Jaidon Weedon (10)

Once Upon A Witch

Once upon a time,
There was a witch covered in grime
She gave a boy a poison sweet,
That tasted of terrible feet
The boy's name was Bob,
And he shoved the sweet inside his gob
The witch gave a terrible laugh,
When Bob wanted to barf
He felt very sick,
Then he turned into a *chick!*

Chudi Patrick Onwuokwu (8)

Underwater Barbecue

The underwater barbecue was a film no longer
The film was for babies, boring!
Aaargh! Found it!
If you're wondering what I found
I found my underwater barbecue map
If you want a barbecue map
Then look under your desk or bed.

Hibbah Altaf

Wonderful Nature

I love the wind, it is so breezy,
I love dogs even though they make me sneezy,
I love the sea, it is so calm,
I love butterflies in my palm,
I love wasps even though they sting,
I wish bees could sing,
I wish trees could ping.

Keeley Grant

Once Upon A Dream

D reaming of dancing with dazzling Darcey
R eaching for a rhythmical repertoire
E nergised by the excitement of the exercise
A bility, agility, attitude and ambition
M ake musical movements magical.

Carys Hunt

Flying Dragons

Five baby dragons were flying,
Lying in the sky
They fell into a black hole
Which was as big as a cereal bowl
Discovering Cookie Crumble Land.

Terence Noble

A Baby Dragon

A fire-breathing dragon called Snuggles
Really loves hugs and cuddles
It is as small as a hat
And is also as fat as a cat.

Tyler Dunn

A Crazy Footballer

Mirror, mirror on the wall
AJ is the best of them all
He headers the ball fifty times
And then he climbs up a brick wall.

AJ Yates

Bonbon The Dancer

I wished on a star,
That I would go far
In a world of sweet imagination
Something fell from the sky
That looked like a spy
But I couldn't make out what it was
It shot down quicker,
Eating a Snicker
Wearing a pair of socks
Oh no! It couldn't be,
Wait, what?
She's in a tree,
It's my cat, Bonbon!
She fell on my head,
Pretending to be dead
And started talking words
She let out a mumble
Like a cookie crumble
I asked her what she meant
She said, "Meow power is always the answer,"
And started becoming a dancer
She jumped up so high, she turned into a fly
And started buzzing away

She flew around a bend,
And that is the end!
Georgia Wilson (10)
Anahilt Primary School, Hillsborough

Rachel The Rainbow

Rachel the rainbow danced up to the sky,
But the question she asked was why,
They need me now but not then
Oh, I know, they should buy a hen
You see the sun and moon
Do not exist in this land
I know you must think I'm a loon
Only the rainbow wakes you up when they want you
But Rachel said, "I'm fed up of being treated like poo!"
So the world went raven-black
But they were saved by the Big Mac
Who never let them down
Wait, hold on, he dropped the pan
Bang! Oh, it's on my head
I think I'm dead
Bye!

Abigail Weatherhead (10)
Anahilt Primary School, Hillsborough

Once Upon A Dream

Once upon a dream,
I was eating ice cream
When my dog Buddy said,
"Why are you sitting in bed?"
My bed was purple and blue
"Well, what do you think I should do?"
"Let's go to the beach."
"Okay, but let me get a peach."
The sea was calm,
"Look, I see a clam!"
The sun was smiling down,
There stood a horse
The sea was going *splish, splash, splosh!*
Someone was riding the horse!
Oh, it was my friend, Katie
So I hopped on
And we rode along the sea's edge.

Olivia Margaret Dodds (11)
Anahilt Primary School, Hillsborough

Tigers

The big majestic creatures
Rule the jungle floor
And if you listen carefully,
You can hear their mighty roar
If you're in the jungle,
Please be careful
I have a hunch
If you let your guard down,
You could be their next lunch
They have no shops,
Or restaurants to go get a meal
They need to hunt so carefully,
To get a nice big deer
They eat meat
Such as pigs, sheep and gazelles
They only eat meat
And sometimes something with a shell.

Cassidy McMullan (10)
Anahilt Primary School, Hillsborough

Unicorns!

Unicorns live in a faraway land
That land is called Uniland,
The unicorns shine as bright as the stars
They smell like cotton candy
Their wings flutter as beautifully
As the soft wind blowing the beautiful flowers
Their horns spray out rainbows
Butterflies fly around their hooves
Their tails are baby pink
The elegant sky in the evening, all pretty pink
I'm speechless because there are much, much more.

Ellie Sloan (9)
Anahilt Primary School, Hillsborough

Sweetie Land

In Sweetie Land,
Everything is made of sweets
Like a little child's dream
My house is made of sweets and chocolate
It has doughnut windows with toffee walls
Although, don't go too close or you will get stuck!
Just wait, I heard something,
"Arghh!" A big elephant is charging,
Right towards my house!
Bang!
Oh no, I'm squashed!

Dawn Erwin (10)
Anahilt Primary School, Hillsborough

Strange Animals

There's something strange in Dreamland,
I don't know what to do
The cows snort like pigs,
And the ducks are playing tig
The cats have no fear,
And the bears are drinking beer
My house is made
From rakes and cakes
The animals are acting strange
I don't know what to do
I need to find a solution, quick,
Before it's too late!

Matthew Patterson (9)
Anahilt Primary School, Hillsborough

Dream Land

In Dream Land,
The day only lasts six hours
And people run to get around
Instead of using cars
The sun in Dream Land has rollerskates
That's why it goes so quickly
And the moon it hates
There are lots of crisps beside the road,
Which are often dinner for a rather hungry chirping toad
That goes *ribbit, ribbit* beside the road.

Henry Houston (9)
Anahilt Primary School, Hillsborough

The Different World

The sky is the ground and the grass is the sky,
The birds chirp at our feet
The eagles are sour meat
Our houses are made from cocoa bricks
And gigantic ice cream tips
Trees are made from candy canes and apple strips
There are no limits, no heights, no fears, no frights
There are crazy monsters and frightful birds
But that's my world.

Rachel Douglas (9)
Anahilt Primary School, Hillsborough

I Want To Be A Gymnast

I want to be a flexible gymnast
As good as I can be
No crack, crack, cracking
No, none of that for me!
Do it all day long
No stop, stop, stopping,
No, not for me!
I am as elegant as a swan
With a smile like the sun
People watch me do gymnastics
They clap, clap, clap
When I am done
What a performance
I have done!

Erin Burns (9)
Anahilt Primary School, Hillsborough

My Dreamland

I tumble and do tricks,
On the bouncy tumble track
One round of two back handsprings
Three backflips
I finally get my routine down
And now... balance beam

I'm on the skinny beam,
I wobble and shake
Nearly fall off but I recover fast
One cartwheel and I round off
Off the beam

Oh, what a dream!

Ellie Wright (10)
Anahilt Primary School, Hillsborough

Dreamland

In Dreamland, time goes slower and you get older
The Earth gets smaller and you get taller
The sun gets colder
The moon gets hotter
On Earth, the grass is blue and the sky is green
The stars are black and space is white
There is no gravity,
So rain goes up and clouds come down
And finally, dogs purr and cats growl.

Nathan Mitchell (9)
Anahilt Primary School, Hillsborough

Fleas

One day, Doctor Dee wanted to have a flea
So he sang, "Dodee!"
All the way to the pet shop
As soon as he went in,
He saw the flea he was looking for
A stray flea buzzing around the room
But he had to pay a fee
So he went home without the flea
But the flea followed him all the way home
And became his pet.

Jacob Wilson (10)
Anahilt Primary School, Hillsborough

Dreamland

In Dreamland, you can be whatever you want to be,
If you don't believe it, then follow me!
You could be a guinea pig who munches on stars,
Or even a cowboy who travels afar
Even origami would be cool
Or maybe even a singing mule!
Believe me now?
Maybe not, well you should
Right there on the spot!

Camilla McMullan (9)
Anahilt Primary School, Hillsborough

Oh What A Dream

The sun will shine when I will smile,
When I mumble, the clouds will rumble
I will eat apple crumble,
With a bumblebee on top
My brothers, Jay, Luke and Rory,
Jumping up and down like ballerinas
While I'm rolling around with laughter

Oh, what a dream!

Oliver Kinnear (10)
Anahilt Primary School, Hillsborough

My Dream House

My house is made of caramel ice cream,
The windows made of ice,
And doors made of cake,
A roof of rock candy,
With towers made of sweets
The tower roof is made of icing swirls,
The garden has a lemonade fountain,
With frogs that talk and have Winder tongues.

Cian Suitor (8)
Anahilt Primary School, Hillsborough

A Dancer

I want to be an elegant dancer,
To dance as elegantly as a swan
No thump, thump, thumping
As I dance all day long
The theatre full of people
Bright lights light the stage
Flowers dance through the air like dancers
I could dance all day long.

Tilly Vaughan (9)
Anahilt Primary School, Hillsborough

Dream Land

Riding on a beach,
On a lovely sunny day
Galloping away,
As fast as lightning
I can see the sun brightening
The water goes *splish, splash, splosh*
As the horse is talking
She's making hoof prints
In the golden dusty sand.

Katie Rutherford (10)
Anahilt Primary School, Hillsborough

Sweet Land

One day I woke up in Sweet Land,
Smelling toffee and caramel
And all the sweet things
You could imagine
The chocolate door
Salted toffee walls
Chocolate caramel floor
And a cotton candy duvet
Oh, if only this wasn't a dream.

Thomas Reid (10)
Anahilt Primary School, Hillsborough

My Dreamland

I gallop and canter
On a sunny day
Water goes *splish, splash, splosh*
On the beach
We make hoof prints
On the silky sand
As we go along
We gallop as fast as lightning
When the horse is talking.

Caitlyn Gillian Patterson (10)
Anahilt Primary School, Hillsborough

Country Road

One sunny day,
There was a car
Going as quick as lightning
Down the country road
As the sky was smiling down
And everything was bright
And that's alright.

Rauri Liam Toland (10)
Anahilt Primary School, Hillsborough

Big Black Dog

B ig black dog
I n the living room
G rowling at me

B ig dog of doom
L ying in a heap
A red eye flaring
C laws are huge
K ing of scaring

D oes he scare you?
O nly in the night
G rowling, glaring, so I'll put up a fight!

Mia Hegarty (9)
Ballymagee Primary School, Bangor

Once Upon A Dream

I dream of going to the States
This is where my dream awaits
I wish to become an actor on stage
And turn over a brand-new page
I'm eleven years old
And cannot wait to see
What this new chapter has planned for me

One day I will move to Hollywood
Where I will hire an agent who is very good
He will get me the role I desire
A new set of skills I'm bound to acquire
If I succeed I will be glad
Because this is the dream I've always had.

Henry Graeme Crowther (11)
Bright Futures School, Greenacres

Football

F ootball is fantastic
O h, I do love football!
O n Saturday, I dreamt of football
T ogether, we played in Old Trafford
B ut in the second half, we got beaten
A nd Jesse Lingard scored a goal
L ike a dream, I scored too!
L oved the match.

Reece Orr (10)
Brookfield Special School, Moira

The Ferrari

F ast as lightning, it speeds up
E verybody loves to watch me driving the Ferrari
R eally brilliant, it's a good car
R acing a Jeep, I won
A Ferrari's faster than a Jeep
R aces on tracks
I love the race.

Charlie Irwin (10)
Brookfield Special School, Moira

The Midnight Clown

One night there was a camping trip but I lost my way in the forest. What a mistake I made coming here on my own.
When I reached a clearing in the middle of the woods, in the distance I could see a big building. It appeared to be a theatre. It started to rain so I went to the building for shelter. I heard some footsteps. I crept upstairs, it was only a mouse. Then I turned to see a clown just standing there, watching me with a grin.
I turned to run, but the doors slammed shut. There was nowhere to run. I was scared stiff. I wanted to scream, but I couldn't. I was frozen to the spot while the clown walked up to me laughing a deep, blood-curdling laugh. I started to sweat when he was right in my face...

Daniel Thomas Lloyd (10)
Corran Integrated Primary School, Larne

The Darkness Of The Day

Smoke, smoke everywhere
Up my nose and in my hair
Rising as black as can be
I can hardly see

I wonder if there's anyone there
Though I don't care, I'm just wondering
Hoping to find someone like you,
Claire McHugh

Amongst the trees and the flowers
Igniting all of my powers
I've never felt so free
Having you here with me

Suddenly, I find a sinister chair,
As the fumes blow through my hair
I wake up from this horrible dream,
Thank goodness it isn't all that it seems.

Lucy O'Cleary (10)
Corran Integrated Primary School, Larne

Professor Wizardy Wizard

Professor Wizardy Wizard was a very wise old chap,
His magnificent white beard left everyone tipping their caps!
But one day, the professor left the country and didn't come home
Until one gloomy night, he came back with a gnome!
Professor Wizardy Wizard was very happy with his new friend
Leaving the people of the country, wondering when it would end
Little did they know the professor was covering things up
Because the professor's gnome was really a painted cup.

Evelyn Donnelly (10)
Corran Integrated Primary School, Larne

A Firework Dream

I dreamt of...

Enchanting planets exploding, illuminating the night
Swiftly soaring spectacular blooming bouquets
Fireworks flying across the sky, painting vibrant primroses
Drawing enchanting shapes in the empty air

I could hear the zooming and the squealing, fiery flames
Spinning tornadoes crashing like a meteor
Banging, crackling and popping onto a starry night canvas
Rockets rapidly racing like cars on the track

Explosive splatters of galactical, enchanting paint
Gargantuan flames of breathtaking, blazing fire glimmering like glistening gold
Neon lines burning down plain, grey clouds
Explosions of joy, blooming blossoms of paint drawing faces on many watching

I dreamt of the most jaw-dropping, delightful sight.

Isabella Sophia Cantrill Taylor (9)
Field View Primary School, Bilston

A Firework Dream

I dreamt of...
Splatters of happiness invading a sad soul of darkness
The hollow sky giving the moon a bouquet of vibrant primroses
Blooming flowers on a black meadow,
Colours exploding in the sky, spreading joy
Masterpieces on a pitch-black painting
Paint being splattered randomly by God
Sparklers blasted in the sky

I could hear the bangs from the gunpowder
Explosions like glass shattering
Crackling from the flames like a fire being put out
Whizzing, zooming, booming, shooting
Sounds of awe coming from spectators
Phones clicking because of people taking pictures

Twisting like tornadoes,
Fluttering like butterflies
Dancing emotionally
Drawing shapes in the sky
Flying up so high
Doodling on the friendly sky
Hiding the stars

Hopping like rabbits
Blooming like blossom

That's our brilliant, enchanting display.

Sirafima Bubnovska (9)
Field View Primary School, Bilston

A Firework Dream

I dreamt of...
Vibrant colourful rockets shooting across the sky,
Blasting a colourful rainbow
Colourful rockets scribbled across the dark sky
Splashes of colourful paint painted like an artist
And burst like a balloon
Blooming blossoms of colourful sparks
Glimmering in the night
Fireballs racing across the sky
With a bang of colourful rainbows

I could hear crackling like a log in a fire,
I could hear banging grenades and powerful guns
There were sounds like popping balloons
Some were popping like popcorn

They were racing like racing cars in a race
They danced like ballerinas skipping through the air
like children
They were fluttering like fluttering butterflies

What a fabulous dream I dreamt of.

Marlon Dalton Bowen (9)
Field View Primary School, Bilston

A Firework Dream

I dreamt of...
Fireworks lighting up the sky
Fireworks were cracking in the sky high up

I could hear the bangs of the fireworks
The fireworks were shooting through the sky
Like shooting stars at night
They were popping like popcorn,
Making the sky all beautiful
The colours of fireworks were creating a rainbow in the sky
They were like diamonds blazing throughout the sky
Cracking up high
I dreamt of stars coming from the galaxy
The enchanting planets exploring
Bright diamonds, blazing fire splatters of enchanting paint
The sounds were like shattering glass
They moved like racing cars, racing in the sky
They fluttered like butterflies
And zoomed like shooting stars.

Trey Smith (9)
Field View Primary School, Bilston

A Firework Dream

I dreamt of...
Glistening colours dancing in the sky,
Sparkles of vibrant fireworks in the night
Dazzling and glimmering all through the night
Drawing shapes in the empty air
Illuminating the sky

I could hear the exploding fireworks
Booming into the night sky
Squealing, crackling into the darkness
Rockets racing like cars on a track

Jumping like kangaroos in the navy blue sky
Explosions of vibrant colours creating a rainbow
Enormous flames of blazing fire, shimmering like diamonds
Fragments of light wriggling through the clouds
Explosions of funny faces blazing in the sky

I dreamt of the most magical, enchanting sight.

Evie Cart (8)
Field View Primary School, Bilston

A Firework Dream

I dreamt of...
Vibrant colourful paint dancing across the black canvas,
Magical flakes of fire were rising into the heavens
It seemed like a human was painting smiles on us
But the popping bubbles couldn't since they were too high up

The squeals and pops of the night sky,
Made the rockets louder and louder
As they exploded more and more
They seemed more and more confident by the second

They were growing, colourful bushes
Powder as sparkly as a diamond covered in glitter
A slow-moving animation on black card
Flames of fire going higher and higher

What I dreamt of was truly the most magical, enchanting sight ever.

Lijana Liutvinskyte (9)
Field View Primary School, Bilston

A Firework Dream

I dreamt of...

Glistening, galactic planets vibrating into the illuminating sky,
Blazing fire exploding like an erupting volcano
Shooting stars splattering like enchanting paint
Sharp spears dancing across the dull night sky

Banging gunshots popping like colourful balloons,
Crackling like logs in a flame of coal
Squealing like whistles on a football pitch
Sizzling like sausages on a hot BBQ

Fluttering like butterflies in the empty air
Zooming shooting stars popping like popcorn
Spinning like a tornado in the dull sky
Dancing elegantly like ballerinas in the sky

I dreamt of the most magical, enchanting sight.

Wiktoria Oliwia Jaramek (9)
Field View Primary School, Bilston

A Firework Dream

I dreamt of...

Vibrant fire exploding into rainbow sparkles to fill the dark sky,
Satisfying colours spinning like crazy
Shining and dazzling during the night
Creating shapes in the darkness
Brightening up the sky

I could hear the banging and screeching of the colourful glows
A sea of vibrant colours
Mesmerising colours spinning like tornadoes
Bright colours screaming as they go in the sky

Exploding of magnificent colours always making rainbows
Gargantuous flames shining bright like a diamond
Vibrant colours blowing people's minds
Racing like rockets in the sky

It was the best sight I had ever seen.

Adrian Philip Brzezinski (9)
Field View Primary School, Bilston

A Firework Dream

I dreamt of…
Bright colours twirling and swirling around,
Sparkles in excitement
Glittering and glimmering in the pitch-black tunnel
Travelling around the moody sky
Like a coloured aeroplane
Coloured dandelion clock getting blown by the unique sky

I could hear fireworks banging and banging in anger
Flying to the black canvas waiting to get painted
The enthusiastic fireworks exploding like a volcano
Fireworks gasping and *bang!*

Fireworks exploding to turn into pom-poms
The fireworks spitting fire out to hurt people
Vibrant fireworks comforting the sad night

I dreamt of the most magical thought.

Debina Chander (9)
Field View Primary School, Bilston

A Firework Dream

I dreamt of...
Velvety primroses being created in the dark, gloomy sky
Galactic planets exploding in the thin air
Fireworks popping like gigantic bubbles
Paint being splattered on the gloomy sky
Flames being launched into the air
Like a rocket ship going to space
Fireworks making gunshot sounds
In the dark, gloomy air
Fireworks crackling like a log in flames
Fireworks exploding like a flare being shot into the air
Fireworks moving like shooting stars in the dark, gloomy sky
Fireworks moving like a tornado
Fireworks moving as if they were skydiving

I dreamt of the most delightful fireworks in the universe.

Izan Duque (9)
Field View Primary School, Bilston

A Firework Dream

I dreamt of...

A brilliant, beautiful display
A universe getting bombed with colours across the sky
Galactic colours of the vibrant galaxy
Orange, golden shooting stars flying through the sky

Exploding like grenades,
Crackling like a log under flames,
Booming like meteors crashing,
Banging volcano erupting,
Popping balloons

Dancing across the night sky,
Splashing vibrant splodges across the galactic galaxy
Whizzing fireworks skipping in mid-air
I dreamt of the most enchanting, magical sight
Dancing elegantly throughout the sky

I dreamt of the most dazzling, glimmering sight.

Sukhraj Jakhu (9)
Field View Primary School, Bilston

A Firework Dream

I dreamt of...
Vibrant colours splattered everywhere in the sky
Sparklers sizzling in the sky like a bee
Glamorous, dazzling fireworks splattered everywhere like paint

I could hear the banging, sizzling and hissing of fireworks in the night sky
The fireworks zoomed into the sky and banged
The fireworks exploded like a gun

Popping like popcorn, fireworks popped into the sky
Diamonds, fireworks shone like the sun
Banging like a drum, the fireworks banged and sizzled in the sky
Fireworks were whizzing yet dancing towards the night sky

I dreamt of the most magnificent, enchanting sight.

Jannati Robia (9)
Field View Primary School, Bilston

A Firework Dream

I dreamt of...
Vibrant colours exploding in the sky like a rainbow
Shooting stars in the sky
Flames are like diamonds flying in the sky
Fireworks shooting in the magical night
The fireworks are like galaxies

The fireworks are making loud explosions in the sky,
The sound is like the cars are racing on the track
They are dancing,
The explosions going in the sky
Like rocks racing like cars on a track

The movements are like a blanket of colours in the sky,
The fireworks are like an individual volcano exploding in the sky
And the meteor crashing in the sky, like a plane.

Veerjyot Singh (9)
Field View Primary School, Bilston

A Firework Dream

I dreamt of...
Shimmering pom-poms and vibrant splatters of paint
Illuminating the dark, ink-black night
The clumsy little ashes tumbling and toddling everywhere
Like inept, minute babies crawling around in the pitch-black sky

I could hear fireworks spitting ash and cackling gurgles from below,
Sparklers swishing and swizzing and constant wowing
The bronze, bright stars were shooting over my head,
They were different and vibrant colours
Some were magenta, lime-green and some were fiery and blood-red
I dreamt of the most unbelievable and fantastic night.

Sofia Bubnovska (9)
Field View Primary School, Bilston

A Firework Dream

I dreamt of...
Galactic stars exploding like a rainbow blanket
Explosions of twenty confetti cannons going off all at the same time
Shooting stars falling from the night sky
Above all of us on this very night

I could hear crackling of sparklers roaring in the night sky,
The banging of the rockets going to the extinction of life
In fact, I heard the best thing ever

They danced like elegant little ballerinas
They hopped, they spun and they ran
As they leapt into the tranquil, elegant sky

I had an astonishing night!

Tyreece Davis (9)
Field View Primary School, Bilston

A Firework Dream

I dreamt of...
Multicoloured bath bombs fizzing in the sky,
They were like colourful aeroplanes flying high
Dancing in the sky like disco lights
Flying higher than a turtle-designed kite

They sound like rockets blasting into space,
Who will be the fastest in the race?
Colourful gunshots making patterns across the sky
Is it a stripe that could fly?

I saw a tiny glistening dot,
I tried to catch it in my pot
I didn't see what other people could see,
Will it ever come back to me?

It was the most magical dream.

Gurparteek Singh Shergill (9)
Field View Primary School, Bilston

A Firework Dream

I dreamt of...
Vibrant primroses painting pictures in the sky,
Shooting stars flying in the night with explosions,
Sparkles drawing pictures in the empty air
Illuminating the darkness

I could hear banging, exploding, sizzling
Fireworks glistening like galaxy stars,
Spinning like a tornado, popping like popcorn,
Zooming like shooting stars

Blazing fire dancing elegantly like a ballerina,
Bright, vibrant diamonds racing like racing cars
Booming blossoms of light cover the night sky

I dreamt of the most enchanted, magical sight.

Tallia Jane Lewis (9)
Field View Primary School, Bilston

A Firework Dream

I dreamt of...
Vibrant colours dazzling and glimmering like colourful bombs,
Gold, shiny balls rapidly zooming across the sky
A rainbow glass that has been shattered in the gloomy night sky
Sparklers spinning and twisting across the night sky

Fireworks banging and screeching,
People in amazement
Hearing thunder as they zoom across the sky

Exploding bath bombs in a dark, black bath
Paint splatters roaming the charcoal-black canvas
Rainbow sand shooting red-hot lava
Enormous flames blazing fire like a diamond.

Kelsie Lydia Shirley (8)
Field View Primary School, Bilston

A Firework Dream

I dreamt of...
Vibrant galactic paintballs shooting in the sky
Bright, shiny diamonds shining like gold in the air
Luminous flames shooting in the air
Illuminating the sky

I could hear them spinning like tornadoes
Meteors crashing like cars hitting a blanket of darkness
They were popping like popcorn
Exploding like bombs

Jumping like kangaroos in the navy blue sky
They were spinning like tornadoes
They were flying in a void
Painting smiles on the faces

I dreamt of an astonishing sight.

Ammaar Binasif (9)
Field View Primary School, Bilston

A Firework Dream

I dreamt of...
Vibrant bath bombs blasting through the sky
Dancing, twisting and flying by
Dazzling, glistening and making pom-poms
Glorious, blazing, colourful bomb-bombs

I can hear the whizzing of the flames,
As they celebrate a lot of names
Colourful just like a rainbow
Beautiful like a paradise bow

They look like spitting flecks of lava,
And they are like a volcano, marva
Shooting through the charcoal night,
Booming with a bit of a fright!

I dreamt of the most magical sight ever.

Lexi Pearson (9)
Field View Primary School, Bilston

A Firework Dream

I dreamt of...
Colourful, vibrant splatters of paint in the air
Exploding crystals in the night sky
The splatters of paint were as bright as a light
Illuminating the dazzling sky

I could hear,
Banging and whizzing of the flames
Popping like popcorn
I heard crackling, zooming and squealing

They were dancing like ballerinas in the night sky,
Exploding colourful paintballs
Zooming, racing like race cars
Flying up like race cars

I dreamt of the most beautiful, magical, amazing sight.

Emilija Zurauskaite (9)
Field View Primary School, Bilston

A Firework Dream

I dreamt of...
Vibrant colours twisting through the gloomy sky,
They travel like multicoloured aeroplanes up high
Sparkles sizzling and twisting
The fireworks are glistening

I can hear the explosions of fireworks
It sounds like when you slurp
Rockets are racing on a track
Which goes *crack, crack, crack!*

Explosions of colourful, metallic bright splatters like paint
It sometimes look faint
They look like pigment
Flying over

I dreamt of the most magical, enchanting sight.

Paige Parkes (9)
Field View Primary School, Bilston

A Firework Dream

I dreamt of...

Multicoloured pom-poms which were lights
Banging and booming, always at night
Glistening aeroplanes dancing and running
Through the blue sky
Rocket ships going into space
Fireworks flashing in the race
Fireworks spitting like a fountain
The volcano is as high as a mountain
Exploding bombs and fizzing bath bombs
Shaped like Mickey Mouse
Beautiful patterns across the sky,
Splatters of paint on a kite
Flecks of fire that are up high
Magical, glorious and enchanted light!

Hareet Kaur Randhawa (9)
Field View Primary School, Bilston

A Firework Dream

Fireworks dancing like Flamenco dancers from Spain
It's a glorious, colourful koala face
It is beautiful, amazing and insane
Outstanding and not a disgrace.

They sound like spears falling from the sky
Also booming and banging
It is amazing and no one would sigh
In the sky they are dangling and hanging.

They look like supersonic eye-catching jets
They swiftly climb to the galaxy
Everyone always placing bets
It's a vibrant-coloured anarchy.

Cobey Dean (9)
Field View Primary School, Bilston

A Firework Dream

Fireworks joyfully dancing in the air
While everyone will stare
They were screaming
And gleaming
Also, their colours were beaming

The sound of fireworks made me amazed
Then we looked up and gazed
We heard squeals, pops and bangs
Oh, and then orangutans
They sounded like rockets, cannons and an RPG

It looked like paint was splattered
Or it was shattered
It was like dandelions in the night sky
But then you had to say goodbye
Sigh.

Nihal Dhaliwal (9)
Field View Primary School, Bilston

A Firework Dream

I dreamt of...
Satisfying colours filling the sky
Amazing, exciting sights of vibrant primroses
Rockets flying high
Shining bright like diamonds

I could hear zooming flying high up
Banging lights on an invisible blanket
Crackling like flames on a log
Popping like popcorn

Spinning like a roller coaster
Dancing like a street dancer
Skipping through the air
Fireworks shooting up

It was an enchanting, life-changing sight.

Jugraaj Kler (9)
Field View Primary School, Bilston

A Firework Dream

I dreamt of…
Vibrant, jaw-dropping fireworks zooming in the pitch-black sky,
In the midnight sky, we are watching them, how they fly

They sound brilliant, astonishing
And they sound like sausages sizzling in a pan
They sound like popcorn popping in a big, multicoloured can

As it was a dancer dancing beautifully,
Twisting and twirling
And they are very artistic
And they are booming like bombs.

Grace Parsons (9)
Field View Primary School, Bilston

A Firework Dream

Fireworks blasting to their nemeses
Like a rocket-propelled grenade
As the vibrant coloured X-4 Stormwing
Is storming into the darkness
Fireworks prance like a fox

A firework explosion as loud as a T-rex
Fireworks showing freedom as they zoom in the air

A bubbly volcano eruption,
Fizzing all the way to space
Elated and breathless until the fun ends.

Zechariah Parkash (9)
Field View Primary School, Bilston

A Firework Dream

I dreamt of…
Fireworks exploding in the sky,
Blue, yellow and green rainbows in the sky

Shooting fireworks to the sky,
Exploding fireworks in space

Loud fireworks to the space explosion
Fireworks rapidly shooting into space

Fireworks exploding in the sky,
Pink and purple in the sky.

lovondeep (8)
Field View Primary School, Bilston

A Firework Dream

I dreamt of...
Fireworks popping like popcorn
Fireworks drawing faces in the night sky

I dreamt of...
Fireworks dancing like a ballerina
Fireworks racing like racing cars in the sky
They jumped like kangaroos
They zoomed like shooting stars
I had an amazing, beautiful night.

Lloyd Harmitt (9)
Field View Primary School, Bilston

A Firework Dream

The fireworks are like emeralds and rubies
The fireworks are like volcanoes exploding
The fireworks are like rockets blasting through the sky
The fireworks are like rockets falling from the sky
They look like something from Mickey Mouse.

Brendan Frost (9)
Field View Primary School, Bilston

The Terror File!

I'm running down the street,
With my heart bounding to the beat
I was grabbed from underneath
With razor-sharp teeth
And brought to a new world inside
I was in a smelly sewer
I couldn't get out any sooner
I was petrified so I sighed
But suddenly I was grabbed from behind
I found out it was my worst nightmare,
Clowns!
He tried to eat me
But I crawled out of the sewer
I closed my eyes in dread
To find myself awake in my bed
I fell back asleep and saw a clown in front of my face
I suddenly felt I had no space
And the clown looked at me in disgrace

I never thought I would say this,
But I ran rapidly away
Even though I knew it was a dream,
I ran away and screamed for help.

Ewan Anthony Pinkett (8)
Harlowbury Primary School, Old Harlow

A Magical Den

In a dainty den of candyfloss in the sky,
My family and I lie
On the ground of sheep wool
With dreamy dancers' posters on the wall
My brother who is two is teething on a shoe
Because his teeth are growing but it's not flowing well
While he's prancing, I'm dancing for it is my dream

But *patter, patter!* It's beginning to rain,
Now I'm falling, feel my heart, it's beating fast
I don't think I'm going to last
Though for some strange reason, I want to dance

So I do
Bang! Kapow!
Eagles everywhere swiftly swoop
They've saved us all!
Now when I'm in trouble,
I know who to call!

Taliah Rufuse (8)
Harlowbury Primary School, Old Harlow

The Lovely Unicorn With The Metallic Horn

A unicorn with a metallic horn
Glows in the glimmering light
But another unicorn hugged the unicorn too tight
Then the sun set and she went to bed
With his toy pet
Then they woke up
And did a bet
For the park or the human-sized cotton candy machine
But the machine won
But they ate a bun first
Because they love eating them
When the toy and the unicorn got there
The unicorn started flying in the machine
Then they went home with a bone
When they got back, they snuggled into bed
With another toy called Fred
They read a story
And then they were off to bed.

Mia Brady (7)
Harlowbury Primary School, Old Harlow

Unicorns Above The Clouds

I found a glistening puddle with sparkles in it, so with a splash, I jumped in and with a boom, I found myself above the clouds! There were dogs on logs, all the cats were sat on the clouds and unicorns shooting stars out of their horns! My eyes sparkled in excitement and joy, I was also jumping up and down! I also touched the soft, fluffy clouds.

A few minutes later, the dogs and cats started twisting and turning, the unicorns covered my eyes because it was weird!

After a few hours, the unicorns opened up the portal so I could go home. I felt a bit upset but happy because I was back!

Cherry Perez-Dusza (8)
Harlowbury Primary School, Old Harlow

Magic Unicorn

M y magic unicorn on a private plane
A tiny spark from nowhere
G igantic, enormous canes!
I know we landed at a palace
C an I find a rascal?

"U hh, what is this?" I say
N eigh! Neigh! Neigh!
I can see a wonderful disco here
C an it be so near?
O h, oh there it is!
R eally, it is here, my magical unicorn, dance, dance, dance!
N ow it's done, let's fly back to our shack

Amazing unicorn!

Lacey Blackshaw (8)
Harlowbury Primary School, Old Harlow

Sky High!

Once I was in the dreamy sky
And I was extremely high
Then I looked beside me
And saw fluffy unicorns and pugs and rabbits
The pretty pugs liked to have hugs
The rabbits had a few habits
And finally, the unicorns had beautiful
Shimmering and shiny horns
Then we all went to space
And then we had a race
And had some delicious ice cream
And it was very nice

Then we flew away
On the unicorns and it was okay
Then we had some more yummy ice cream!

Renee Firth-Moon (7)
Harlowbury Primary School, Old Harlow

Monsters And Dragons Everywhere!

I am in a gloomy forest
With my family
Feeling worried and scared
Because dragons are breathing fire at me!

Suddenly, a dirty dragon
Whoosh! I was out of control
I thought I was dreaming,
We were not in Dark Forest anymore

M erry monsters and
O val monsters
N anny dragons
S limy monsters
T ired dragons
E lderly dragons
R are monsters
S andy monsters.

Evie Beeson (8)
Harlowbury Primary School, Old Harlow

The Battle Of Cotton Candy Land

I went on a stroll in Cotton Candy Land
I was a bit scared so I needed a hand
I heard a bang, so me and Taliah prepared for battle
I think it's easy but it's quite a hassle
I see a magical unicorn with wings I want to ride
The fire and bombs scare me so I hide
The battle is done, I'm finally free
I can live life how I want to be

I want to live life happily,
Because the battle was terrifying and glorious.

Faith Hinga (8)
Harlowbury Primary School, Old Harlow

The Flamingo Corn

A unicorn horn on a pink flamingo
Glimmering in the moonlight
Flying in the rainbow candyfloss sprinkle clouds
Since the flamingo corn
Was hungry
She decided to eat some!
She ate some
And well, here comes the funny part,
She pooped out
Lots of sprinkles!

She found a Bobocorn
So she opened it
And she got a flamingo corn
Just like herself.

Ella-Rose Jackson (8)
Harlowbury Primary School, Old Harlow

Est.1991

YOUNG WRITERS INFORMATION

We hope you have enjoyed reading this book – and that you will continue to in the coming years.

If you're a young writer who enjoys reading and creative writing, or the parent of an enthusiastic poet or story writer, do visit our website **www.youngwriters.co.uk**. Here you will find free competitions, workshops and games, as well as recommended reads, a poetry glossary and our blog.

If you would like to order further copies of this book, or any of our other titles, then please give us a call or visit **www.youngwriters.co.uk**.

Young Writers
Remus House
Coltsfoot Drive
Peterborough
PE2 9BF
(01733) 890066
info@youngwriters.co.uk